NIRVANA
A STORY OF BUDDHIST PSYCHOLOGY

NIRVANA
A STORY OF BUDDHIST PSYCHOLOGY

BY

PAUL CARUS

ILLUSTRATOINS BY KWASONG SUZUKI

LEARNEST THOU THAT COMPOUND THINGS ARE FLEETING, BRAHMAN, THOU SHALT KNOW THE UNCREATE,
DHAMMAPADA, 383.

GYAN

Published by

Gyan Publishing House
5, Ansari Road
Daryaganj, New Delhi-110002
Phone: 011-47034999, 9811692060
E-mail: books@gyanbooks.com

Distribution Network
gyanbooks.com
India, USA, Canada, UK, Australia, France

ISBN : 978-81-212-3823-6 (PB)
First Published, 1902

2nd Impression 2020

Printed at: Gyan Press, Delhi.

Nirvana
A Story of Buddhist Psychology
Author: Paul Carus

NIRVÂNA

A

STORY OF BUDDHIST PSYCHOLOGY

BY

PAUL CARUS

ILLUSTRATIONS BY KWASONG SUZUKI

LEARNEST THOU THAT COMPOUND THINGS ARE FLEETING,
BRAHMAN, THOU SHALT KNOW THE UNCREATE.

DHAMMAPADA, 383.

CHICAGO
THE OPEN COURT PUBLISHING COMPANY

LONDON AGENTS
KEGAN PAUL, TRENCH, TRÜBNER & CO., LTD.

1902

PREAMBLE.[1]

WHEN Buddha, the Blessed One, the Tathâgata, the great sage of the Sâkya tribe, was yet walking on earth, the news thereof spread over all the valley of the holy Ganga, and every man greeted his friend joyfully and said: "Hast thou heard the good tidings? The Enlightened One, the Perfect One, the holy teacher of gods and men, has appeared in the flesh and is bodily walking among us! I have seen him and have taken refuge in his doctrine; go thou also and see him in his glory. His countenance is beautiful like the rising sun; he is tall and strong like the young lion that has left his den; and when the Blessed One opens his mouth to preach, his words are like music, and all those who listen to his sermons believe in him. The kings of Magadha, of Kôsala, and of many other countries have heard his voice, have received him, and confess themselves his disciples. The Blessed Buddha has solved the riddle of the world and understands the problem of existence. He teaches that life is suffering, but he knows both the origin of suffering and the escape from it, and assures his disciples that Nirvâna can be obtained by walking in the noble path of righteousness."

SUDATTA, THE BRAHMAN YOUTH, AT THE PLOW.

IN the fields of Kuduraghara,[2] a small township of Avanti, there was a tall Brahman youth, by name Sudatta, plowing the grounds of Subhûti, who was called by the people Mahâ-Subhûti because he was wealthy, and whom the king had appointed chief of the village, to be a judge in all cases of law, both for the decision of litigations and the punishment of crimes.

Sudatta, while driving the draught-oxen, was merrily singing. He had good reason to be full of joy, for Mahâ-Subhûti, the chief, had chosen him for his son-in-law, and when, according to an old custom, the youth offered four clods to the maiden, one containing seeds, one ingredients from a cow-stable, one dust from an altar, and one earth taken from a cemetery, she had not touched the clod taken from the cemetery, which would have been an evil omen, but chose the clod containing dust from the altar, indicating thereby that her descendants would be distinguished priests and sacrificers. This was in Sudatta's opinion the noblest and most desirable fate. Rich harvests and prosperity in the raising of cattle were great blessings, but what are all worldly possessions in comparison to the bliss of religion! It was this idea that made Sudatta sing, and he was happy, even as Indra, the strong god, when intoxicated with the sweet juices of sôma.

Suddenly the plow struck the lair of a hare, and the hare jumped up to flee, but turned anxiously back to look after her brood. Sudatta raised the stick with which he goaded his oxen, chased the hare and sought to kill her, and would have accomplished his purpose had he not been interrupted by the voice of a man passing on the highroad, who called out: "Stay, friend! What wrong has that poor creature done?" Sudatta stopped in his pursuit and said: "The hare has done no wrong, except that she lives in the fields of my master."

The stranger was a man of serene appearance, and his shaven head indicated that he

was a samana, a monk, who had gone into homelessness for the sake of salvation. It was Anuruddha, a disciple of the Blessed One.

Seeing the plowman's noble frankness and the beauty of his appearance, he saluted him, and, as if trying to excuse the lad's conduct, the samana suggested: "You probably need the hare's flesh for meat."

"O, no!" replied the youth, "the flesh is not fit to eat in the breeding season. I chased the hare for sheer sport. Hares are quick, and there are but few boys who can outrun them."

"My dear friend," continued Anuruddha, "imagine yourself a parent whom some fierce giant deprived of his children and whom he hunted to death, as you intended to do unto this poor hare!"

"I would fight him," replied Sudatta eagerly, "I would fight him, though he might kill me."

"You are a brave boy," rejoined the samana, "but suppose the giant killed all your loved ones, your father and mother, your wife and children, and left you alive, mocking at your misery."

The youth stood abashed. He had never troubled his mind with such thoughts. He had never cared for creatures weaker than himself, and, for the sake of mere amusement, would not have hesitated to inflict pain on others. He was noble-minded and ambitious, eager to dare and to do, yet in one thing he was wanting.

Anuruddha thought to himself: "This youth is of a noble nature, but ill-advised. Should he remain uninstructed, his uncontrolled energy would do great harm. Would that he understood the religion of the Tathâgata, which is glorious in the letter and glorious in the spirit, true in its foundations, radiant as sunlight in its doctrines, and lofty in its practical applications. His manliness and courage, which would otherwise go to waste, might be turned to accomplish great things." And he addressed Sudatta saying: "Do you not know, friend, the words of the Tathâgata on behavior toward animals? The Blessed One said:

> "'Suffuse the world with friendliness.
> Let creatures all, both mild and stern,
> See nothing that will bode them harm,
> And they the ways of peace will learn.'[3]

"This hare, like all other creatures in the

world, is possessed of sentiments such as you experience. She is, as much as you, subject to pain, old age, and death. You were not always strong and healthy. Years ago you were a tiny and helpless baby, and would not have lived but for the tender care of your loving mother and the protection of your dear father. You think of the present, forgetting your past and reckoning not on your future. As you no longer remember your suckling days, and know nothing of your state when you were safely sheltered in the womb of your mother, so you do not remember former existences in which your character developed in a gradual evolution to its present condition."

"Venerable man," said the youth, "you are a good teacher and I am willing to learn."

The samana continued: "Even the Tathâgata, our Lord, passed through all the stages of life in regular succession. By thoughts of truth, by self-control, and deeds of kindness he so fashioned his heart that he rose in the scale of beings until he became the Enlightened One, the perfect and Holy Buddha, and attained to Nirvâna. Æons ago he started on his earthly career in humble destitution and weakness. As a fish he swam in the ocean, as a bird he lived in the branches of trees and according to his deeds he passed from one form of existence to another. It is said, too, that he was a hare eking out a precarious existence in the fields. Did you never hear the tale?"

"No, never!" replied the youth, "tell me the story."

THE STORY OF THE HARE.[4]

ANURUDDHA began:

"So I have heard: Bôdhisatta[5] once lived as a hare in the fields of a fertile country, and the hares waxed so numerous that food became scarce and they became a plague to the country.

"Then the thought occurred to Bôdhisatta while he was a hare: the times are hard and the people suffer for want of rice and wheat. They will rise in anger and slay all the hares that live in this country, and I, too, will have to die. Can I not do a noble deed lest in this present incarnation I live in vain? I am a weak creature and my life is useless unless I can contribute something, be it ever so little, toward the advance of enlightenment, for through enlightenment alone the bliss of deathless Nirvâna is attained. Let me seek Nirvâna. There is in this world such a thing as efficacy of virtue; there is efficacy of truth. Buddhahood is possible, and those who have attained Buddhahood by the wisdom of earnest thought and good deeds will show to others the path of salvation. The Buddhas' hearts are full of truth and compassion, of mercy and long suffering. Their hearts reach out in equal love to all beings that live. I will imitate them, and I will become more and more like them. The truth is one and there is but one eternal and true faith. It behooves me, therefore, in my meditation on the Buddhas, and relying on the faith that is in me, to perform an act of truth that will advance goodness and alleviate suffering.

"Having meditated on the path of salvation, Bodhisatta decided to warn his brother hares of the coming danger, to point out to them the instability of life, and to teach them the blessings of frugality and abstinence.

'And Bôdhisatta approached his brother hares and preached to them; but they would not listen to his words. They said: 'Go, thou, Brother Bôdhisatta, and perform a noble deed; go thou, and sacrifice thyself for the truth;

die that others may live, and take your chance of being reborn in a higher and better incarnation. But do not inconvenience us with your sermons. We love life and prefer the happiness which we enjoy, and which is real, to the spread of truth, the bliss of which is a mere assumption. There is plenty of maize and wheat and rice and all kinds of sweet fruits in the fields for us to eat. You need not worry about us. Everybody must look out for himself.'

"Now, there was a Brahman who had retired into the woods for the sake of meditating on the attainment of Nirvâna. And the Brahman suffered severely from hunger and cold. He had lit a fire to keep himself warm after a chilly shower; and stretching his hands over the fire he bewailed his lot, saying: 'I shall die before I have finished my meditation, for I must starve for lack of food.'

"Bôdhisatta, seeing the worthy man in need, said to himself: 'This Brahman shall not die, for his wisdom may still be as a lamp to many others who grope in darkness. I will offer myself as food to him.' "With these thoughts in his heart, Bôdhisatta jumped into

the fire offering himself as meat for him and thus rescued the Brahman from starvation.

"Soon afterwards the people of the country, in fear of a famine, prepared a great hunt. They set out all of them, on one and the same day, and drove the hares into a narrow enclosure, and in one day more than a hundred thousand died under the clubs of the hunters."

WHAT IS NIRVÂNA?

WHEN Anuruddha had finished the story of the hare he said to Sudatta: "To live means to die. No creature that breathes the breath of life can escape death. All composite things will be dissolved again. Nothing can escape dissolution. But good deeds do not die. They abide forever. This is the gist of the Abhidharma. He who dares to surrender to death that which belongs to death, will live on and will finally attain to the blessed state of Nirvâna."

"What is Nirvâna?" asked the youth.

Anuruddha replied by quoting the words of the Great Master, saying:

"When the fire of lust is gone out then Nirvâna is gained.

"When the flames of hatred and illusion have become extinct then Nirvâna is gained.

"When the troubles of mind, arising from

pride, credulity, and all other sins, have ceased, then Nirvâna is gained."

The countenance of the youth betrayed his dissatisfaction with the new doctrines, and the Buddhist continued: "No one who still clings to the illusion of Self can understand, let alone taste, the sweetness of Nirvâna. All temporal existence is transient; all composite things have originated and will be dissolved again; and there is nothing abiding in bodily existence. Every concrete object has been moulded by its causes, and every individual organism has originated in the natural course of evolution, according to the conditions which determine its history. The constituents of being are in a constant flux, and there is nothing that could be regarded as a permanent Self, as an immortal being, as an entity of any kind that would remain identical with itself. Know, then, that which remains identical with itself, that which is eternal, that which is absolutely immutable and permanent, is not a concrete being, not a material body of any description, not a particular and individual existence; not a Self of any kind. And yet it exists! The deathless, the immortal and immutable, is an actuality; it is the most significant and important actuality in the world, but this actuality is spiritual, not substantial. And what is it? The deathless, which in its omnipresence is immutable and eternal, is the Bôdhi; it is the harmony of all those verities that remain the same forever and aye. The truths on which the wise rely when they argue are not particular things, not single facts, not concrete entities, not Selfs of any kind, neither gods nor animate beings; they are nothing—if nothing means the absence of any concrete thingishness or special selfhood; and yet their nothingness is not a non-existence. If the deathless, the immortal, the immutable, did not exist, there would be no escape from the sufferings of the world. If the Bôdhi were an illusion there would be no enlightenment; Nirvâna could not be attained and no Buddha could ever appear to point out the way of salvation. But the Buddha hath appeared; he hath understood the utter groundlessness of the belief in an immutable Self; he hath discovered that all misery consists in the clinging to Self;

and he pointeth out the way of salvation, through the attainment of the Bôdhi, leading all those who honestly seek the light, on the eightfold noble path of righteousness, to the glorious and deathless Nirvâna."

"Venerable man," said Sudatta, "the noble Sâkyamuni of whom you learned the doctrine that you proclaim seems to be a great master; yet he will not be honored in Kuduraghara, for we are all good orthodox Brahmans, and there is not one follower of the Buddha among us. Nevertheless, I must not conceal from you that there is one man in our village who speaks highly of Sâkyamuni. It is Mahâ-Subhûti, a friend of king Bimbisâra, the judge and chief of the township. If you enter the village go to him and he will receive you. Not that he is a follower of the Buddha, but a friend of his by personal attachment, for he has met Gautama[6] at the king's court and he says: 'Should Brahma, the god, ever descend upon earth he would appear like Gautama; for surely Brahma could not look more majestic nor more divine than the noble Sâkyamuni.' When you meet Subhûti, the chief, greet him in my name, in the name of Sudatta, the son of Rôja, and he will invite you to witness the marriage of his daughter, which shall take place to-morrow. Go then to the house of Mahâ-Subhûti, and there I shall meet you, for I am the man to whom his daughter is betrothed."

BEGGING FOR ALMS.

WHEN Anuruddha entered Kuduraghara, the Brahman village on the precipice near Kuduraghara, he hesitated a moment and thought to himself: "What shall I do? Shall I go to Mahâ-Subhûti, or shall I go from house to house according to the rules of the order of samanas?" And he decided: "The rule must be followed. I will not go to Mahâ-Subhûti, but will go from house to house."

With form erect and eyes cast down, holding his bowl in his left hand, the samana placed himself in front of the first house, patiently waiting for alms. As no one appeared at the door, the slender figure moved on. Many refused to give him anything, sending him away with angry words. Even those who offered him a small portion of rice called him a heretic; but as he was free from desire as to his personal concerns, he blessed the donors;

and, when he saw that he had enough to satisfy the needs of the body, he turned back to eat

his modest meal under the green trees of the forest. While crossing the square of the village, there appeared in the door of the town hall a dignified Brahman, who, after a searching glance at the stranger, stopped him and asked: "Art thou a disciple of the Blessed One, the Holy Buddha?"

"I am Anuruddha, a disciple of the Blessed One," replied the samana.

"Well, well," said the Brahman, "I should know you, for I have met the Blessed One at Râjagaha, and he spoke with admiration of Anuruddha[7] as a master in metaphysics and a philosopher who has grasped the doctrine of the Tathâgata. If you are indeed Anuruddha, I welcome you to my house. Do me the honor, O venerable samama, of staying with me at my house; deign to take your meal at my residence. And I shall be glad if you will grace with your presence the marriage of my daughter, which will take place to-morrow."

"Allow me, O chief of Kuduraghara," replied Anuruddha "to eat my meal in the forest, and to-morrow I shall come and witness the marriage of your daughter."

"Be it so!" said Subhûti. "You will be welcome whenever you come."

THE WEDDING.

SUBHÛTI'S mansion was decorated with flags and garlands, and a bridal reception-hut was built of bamboo in the courtyard over the fireplace. The inhabitants of Kuduraghara were waiting at the door to watch the procession.

Sudatta, the groom, appeared in festive attire with his friends and approached reverently the father of the bride. The venerable Brahman chief received the young man cordially and led him to the family altar in the presence of his wife, the bride's mother, and his only son Kacchâyana. There he offered to the groom the honey drink, and presented to his daughter the bridal gown with a costly head ornament and a necklace of jewels.

Addressing the groom he said: "It behooves a Brahman father to select as husband for his daughter, a Brahman maiden of pure caste, a Brahman youth, the legitimate son of Brahman parents, and to marry the couple according to the Brahma-rite. I have chosen thee, O Sudatta, for thou art worthy of the bride. Thou art of Brahman caste, thy bones, thy knees, thy neck, thy shoulders are strong. The hair of thy head is full, thy skin is white, thy gait is erect, and thy voice is clear. Thou art well versed in the Vêda and of good conduct. Thy parents are respected in the village, and I am confident that you will fulfil all the duties of a good husband. My daughter

shall be thy lawful wife, loyal in adversity as well as in good fortune, and may the children that shall be born to thee, and thy children's children, be worthy of their ancestors in the line of either parent. The bride is ready

in her bridal garments. Receive her and perform the duties of life in unison."

The sacrifices were properly performed according to the traditions of the country, and while the highest priest of the village recited the Mantra, the father of the bride poured out

the water libation. The groom clasped the maiden's hand, and she stepped upon the stone of firmness. Then the young couple performed the ceremony of circumambulating the altar in seven steps, indicating that they would henceforth be partners in life and meet all changes of fate, whether good or evil, in unison.

Thereupon the married couple, preceded by the groomsman Kacchâyana, the bride's brother, the bridesmaids, and all the guests, started for the groom's house, the future home of the bride. Fire from the altar on which the burnt offerings had been consumed was carried in an iron pan by a priest who followed the bridal carriage.

While the bridal procession was passing through the street, the people hailed the bride and threw handfuls of rice over her with invocations and blessings. At Sudatta's residence, the groom carried the bride over the threshold. The new hearth fire was lit with the flames of the bridal altar, and when the prescribed sacrifice was made, the young couple circumambulated the holy fire of Agni three times. Then they sat down on the red cowhide spread out before them, and a little boy, a relative of the family, was placed in the bride's lap, while the brother of the groom's deceased father, a venerable old priest, prayed over her: "May Agni, who blazes forth with hallowed flame upon the hearth of the house, protect thee! May thy children prosper and see the fulness of their days! Be thou blessed, O worthy maiden, in thy bridal beauty as a mother of healthy children, and mayest thou behold the happy faces of vigorous sons!"

Then the groom gave a handful of roasted barley to the bride and said: "May Agni bestow blessings upon the union of our hands and hearts!"[8]

A SERMON ON HAPPINESS.

AFTER the completion of the wedding ceremonies, Subhûti invited his guests to partake of a meal, and seeing among the people Anuruddha, the philosopher, he called him to sit at his side. The guests were merry and enjoyed the feast, and when the evening grew cooler and the moon rose in mild radiance, the company sat down under the branches of a large banyan tree and began to speak of the blessings of the gods and the glory of their country. Then Subbûti, the judge, addressed Anuruddha and said:

"Venerable Anuruddha, I cherish a high regard for the Blessed One, the sage of the Sâkyas, whom the people call the Tathâgata, the Holy Buddha. But it seems to me that his doctrine will not suit our people. It is a philosophy for those who are oppressed by the evils of life; it affords a refuge to the weary, the sick, the sorrowing; but with the happy, the powerful, the healthy, it must be a failure. It may be a balm for those that are wounded in the battle, but it is distasteful and like unto poison to the victor."

Said Anuruddha: "The doctrine of the Blessed One is indeed for those who are oppressed by the evils of life. It affords a refuge to the weary, for it secures to them health and happiness. The happy, the powerful, the hale, need no comfort, no assistance, no medicine. But who are hale, happy, and healthy? Is there any one among you free from the liability to sorrow, disease, old age, and death? If so, he might truly be called a victor, and he would not be in need of salvation.

"Now, indeed, I see here much happiness around me. But is your happiness well grounded? Will your minds remain serene and calm in the time of affliction and in the hour of death? He only has attained genuine happiness who has entered the deathless Nirvâna, that state of heart which lifts above the petty temptations of the world and liberates from the illusion of Self. Happiness on account of worldly prosperity is a dangerous condition; for all things change, and he only is truly happy who has surrendered his attachment to things changeable. There is no genuine happiness except it be grounded upon religion, the religion of the Tathâgata.

"The Tathâgata opens the eyes of those who deem themselves happy that they may see the dangers of life and its snares. When the fish perceives the bait he believes he is happy, but he feels his misery as soon as the sharp hook pierces his jaws.

"He who is anxious about his personal happiness must always be full of fear. He may be indifferent to the misery of his fellow-beings, but he cannot be blind to the fact that the same end awaits us all. Happy he who resigns to death that which belongs to death. He has conquered death; whatever be his fate, he will be calm and self-possessed; he has surrendered the illusion of Self and has entered the realm of the immortal. He has attained to Nirvâna."

Sudatta looked at the bride and said: "I shall never embrace Gautama's doctrine, for it would not behoove a groom to leave his bride for the sake of the attainment of Nirvâna."

Anuruddha overheard Sudatta's remark and continued: "My young friend fears that the doctrine of the Tathâgata would tear him away from the bride to whom to-day he has pledged his troth. That is not the case. The Blessed One left his wife and child and went into homelessness because error prevails and the world lies in darkness. Having reached the deathless Nirvâna, he is now bent alone on the one aim of pointing out the path to others, and we, his disciples, who like him have left the world, devote ourselves to a religious life, not for our own sake, for we have released all attachment to Self, but for the sake of the salvation of the world. Our maxim is expressed in the one word *anattavâdo*,[9] the non-assertion of self.

"It is not the severing of the ties of life that constitutes liberation, but the utter surrender of Self. The hermit who has cut himself off from the world but still cherishes in his heart the least inkling of desire, lusting for happiness in this life or in a life to come, is not yet free, while a humble householder, if he has surrendered all craving, may attain that glorious condition of soul, the fruition of which is Nirvâna.

"He who longs for a religious life should leave worldly considerations behind, and apply himself with all his energy to obtain enlightenment. But he who has duties to perform at home should not shirk his responsibility. The Tathâgata says:

"'Cherish father and mother,
And wife and children: this
And love of a peaceful calling,
Truly, is greatest bliss.

"'Practising lovingkindness,
Befriending one's kindred: this
And to lead a life that is blameless,
Truly, is greatest bliss.

"'Self-control and wisdom,
The four noble truths,—all this,
And attainment of Nirvâna,
Truly, is greatest bliss.'"[10]

THE CONTROVERSY.

ANURUDDHA saw that Sudatta was filled with indignation. So he ceased to speak and looked expectantly at the young man. Sudatta rose to his feet and said:

"'Utter surrender of Self?'[11] Is that the liberation which Gautama preaches? My father called him a heretic and an infidel, and truly he was not mistaken, for Gautama's liberation is a destruction: it annihilates man's Self. Gautama rejects the authority of the sacred Scriptures. He does not believe in Îshvara,[12] the Lord of Creation, and he holds that there is no soul. Yea, he is so irreligious that he condemns sacrifices as impious, ridicules prayer as useless, and would fain destroy our sacred institution of castes on which the social order of our civilisation rests. His religion is the negation of all religion, it is not divine but purely human, for it rejects belief in the divinity of the

Vedas and claims that enlightenment is sufficient to illumine the path of life."

Anuruddha listened to Sudatta's vehement denunciations, and observing the heightened color in his cheeks, thought to himself: "How beautiful is this lad and how noble does he appear in his pious zeal for the religion of his father!" Then he said: "The Tathâgata does not oppose Brahmanism. He who has grasped his doctrines will understand that he is a reformer. He revealed to us a higher interpretation of religion."

Replied Sudatta: "A denial of the existence of the Self[13] will destroy all religion."

Anuruddha asked: "What do you mean by Self?"

Sudatta, who was well trained in the Vedânta philosophy, said: "My Self is the immutable eternal Ego that directs my thoughts. It is that which says 'I.'"

"What is the Ego or that which says 'I'?" exclaimed Anuruddha: "There is unquestionably something which says 'I' in me, and in you, and in everybody present. But when we say 'I,' it is a mode of speech, as much as are all the other words and ideas that people our minds. The word 'I,' it is true,

remains the same throughout life, but its significance changes. It originates in the child with the development of self-consciousness, and denotes first a boy, then a youth, after that a man, and at last a dotard. The word may remain the same, but the substance of its meaning changes. Accordingly, that something which says 'I,' is neither eternal, nor immutable, nor divine, nor what Yoga philosophers call 'the real Self.' It is a word which signifies the whole personality of the speaker with all his sensations, sentiments, thoughts, and purposes."

The Brahman replied: "Gautama is an infidel who denies the existence of the soul, and yet is so inconsistent as to talk about rebirth in future incarnations, and of immortality."

"Let us not haggle about words, friend Sudatta," said the samana, "but understand the doctrine aright. The Tathâgata looks upon that assumedly immutable ego-self of which you speak as an error, an illusion, a dream; and attachment to it will produce egotism which is a craving for happiness either here on earth or beyond in heaven. But while that illusory Self is an error of your philosophy, your personality is real. There is not a person who is in possession of character, thoughts, and deeds; but character, thoughts, and deeds themselves are the person. There is not an ego in you, O Sudatta, that thinks your thoughts and shapes your character, but your thoughts themselves are thinking, and your character itself is the nature of your very self. Your character, your thoughts, your volitions are you yourself. You have not ideas, but you are ideas."

"But who is the lord of these ideas of mine?" asked Sudatta. "Here your theory is wanting. Blessed is he who knows that the lord of his ideas is his ego, his Self."

Anuruddha continued: "The ego-idea is not a lord who owns your body and mind, directing the emotions and impulses of your character; but those of your emotions which are the strongest, they are the Lord, they govern you. If evil passions grow in your heart, you will be like a ship which is at the mercy of the winds and the currents of the sea; but if the aspiration for enlightenment takes possession of you, it will steer you to the haven of Nirvâna where all illusions cease and the heart will be tranquil like a still, smooth lake. Deeds are done; and the doing of deeds passes away; but that which is accomplished by deeds abides; just as a man who writes a letter ceases writing, but the letter remains. Considering the permanence that is in deeds, what can be better than shaping our future existence wisely? Lay up a treasure of charity, purity, and sober thoughts. He who lives in noble thoughts and good deeds will live forever, though the body may die. He will be reborn in a higher existence and will at last attain the bliss of Nirvâna. There is no transmigration of a self-substance, but there is a re-incarnation of thought-forms which takes place according to the deeds that are done."

"The Buddha teaches that good deeds should be done vigorously, and only the bad volitions which are done from vanity, or lust, or sloth, or greed, should be eradicated."

Sudatta's belief in the doctrine of the Self was not shaken. No, he felt more assured than ever of its truth, for his whole religion hung on it, and he exclaimed: "What are my deeds without my Self? What is enjoyment if I am not the enjoyer?"

Anuruddha's pensive countenance grew more serious than ever: "Dismiss the craving for enjoyment and all thought of Self and live in your deeds for they are the reality of life. All creatures are such as they are through their deeds in former existences. The thought-forms are the realities of our spiritual life. They are transferred from one individual to another. Individuals die, but their thought-forms will be reincarnated according to their deeds. Deeds shape in the slow process of growth the thought-structures which build up our personality, and that which you call the person, the enjoyer, the Self, is the totality of your thought-forms, the living memory of past deeds. Deeds done in past existences are stamped upon each creature in the character of his present existence. Thus the past has borne the present, and the present is the womb of the future. This is the law of Karma, the law of deeds, the law of cause and effect."

"You take away the unity of the soul," replied Kacchâyana.

"Say rather," rejoined Anuruddha, "I insist upon the complexity and wealth of man's spiritual nature. So long as the illusion of self is upon you, you cannot reach Nirvâna."

The samana's words were weighty and serious. Nevertheless, his auditor remained unconvinced, and Kacchâyana murmured to himself: "Gautama's doctrine cannot be the truth. It would be a sad truth, indeed, if it were true after all. I shall hold fast to the dearest hope of the religion of my father."

The samana replied: "Choose not the dearest but the truest; for the truest is the best."

THE KATHA-UPANISHAD.[14]

SUDATTA was too happy to give himself trouble about the doctrines of a heretical teacher. He would have dismissed all thought of his controversy with Anuruddha, had he not been reminded of it from time to time by his father-in-law and by Kacchâyana, his brother-in-law, who continued to discuss the religious innovations of the Tathâgata. They granted that caste distinctions were hard on the lower castes, but declared that they could not be relaxed without injury to the community, and there was no question about its being a divine institution. Yet it was right to extend our sympathy to all sentient beings that suffer, and the lowest creatures should not be excepted. Certainly we must not by negligence of worship provoke the wrath of the gods; but were the gods truly in need of the bloody sacrifices offered at their altars?

Such were the questions that moved the minds of Subhûti and Kacchâyana; and they

began to doubt while they investigated; yet they remained good Brahmans.

One day Subhûti, the chief of Kuduraghara,

came to his son with a joyful countenance and said: "Kacchâyana, my boy, I trust that I have found the solution of the problem. It

came to me while I was preparing myself for a performance of the Nâchiketas fire-sacrifice, after the manner of the Katha school. While reading the Yajur-Veda, I understood the difficulties and all doubts were resolved. Take leaves from the big palm-tree in our garden, and bleach them, cut off their pointed ends and prepare them for writing. I am eager to give a definite shape to my thoughts before I forget them."

Said Kacchâyana with ardent expectation: "And what in brief is the solution you have arrived at?"

The Brahman chief replied: "Listen, I will tell you. Death is the great teacher of the deepest problems of life. He who wants to know the immortal must enter the house of Death and learn from death the secret of life. There is no child born in this world but is destined to be an offering to Death. Yet Death is not Brahma, he is not the ruler and lord; he portends dissolution but cannot annihilate the soul, and the man who fears him not is granted three boons. Death allows those who enter his house to return and be reborn; he further concedes that the deeds of men shall be imperishable; and lastly he reveals to the courageous inquirer the mystery of life."

Said Kacchâyana: "Profound, O father, are

these thoughts; but the main thing is, What is the lesson Death teaches?"

Subhûti collected his thoughts, and after a pause said: "The doctrine of the Blessed One has deeply affected my mind, but I am not as yet convinced that the fundamental notions of our sacred religion are baseless. Is the great fire sacrifice indeed an empty ceremony that bears no fruit? If it were, our sages would truly be, as says the Sakyamuni, blind leaders of the blind. Sacrifices are without fruit to him only who has not conquered the desires of his heart and has not severed the ties which bind him to that which is transient."

After a brief pause Subhûti continued: "And the idea of an immutable Self cannot be mere fiction. I understand now that the Self is the uncreated and the sole ruler within all things, yet it cannot be seen by the eye, reached by the speech or apprehended by the mind; the Self must be imagined by the heart. The Self is briefly expressed in the exclamation 'Om,' and is the absolute being which is neither born nor dies."

"Your solution, then," continued Kacchâyana, "though a new Brahmanism is a justification of the old?"

"Indeed it is," enjoined Subhûti, "but my attitude is considerably modified by the suggestions of our friend Anuruddha. I grant that that which is good is one thing and that which is dear to our hearts is another thing; and it is well to cling to the good and abandon, for the sake of the better, that which is dear to our hearts. I cannot deny the truth which the Tathâgata impresses upon the minds of his followers, that all compounded things will be dissolved, but I feel in my inmost heart that there is something which death cannot destroy; and it is that which our sages call the Self. I am anxious to know what it is, for only he who knows it will find peace of soul. Let Anuruddha explain to me the problem of the Self, but he must not say that there is nothing that I can call my own, that life is empty, and that the eternal has no existence."

* * *

During the rainy season Subhûti could be seen writing in the shelter of his veranda, and when the sun broke through the clouds and the blue sky reappeared in its former beauty he had his treatise finished, which he called the Katha-Upanishad.

THE IMMORTALITY OF DEEDS.

IT was in these days of the return of good weather that the disciples of the Blessed Buddha were wont to start out on their pilgrimages through the country preaching the glorious doctrine of salvation, and Anuruddha passed again through the village of Avanti while Subhûti sat before his house in the shade of a sala tree reading and reconsidering what he had written. The two men exchanged greetings, and when Anuruddha saw the manuscript, they at once began to discuss the great problem of the Hereafter.

Subhûti read to Anuruddha the Katha-Upanishad, and the venerable monk was greatly pleased with its literary beauty and thoughtfulness, but he shook his head and said: "Truly there is the immortal, but the immortal is not a Self, the immortal is not a being, it is not an entity, nor is it the ego that appears in our perception of consciousness. All things, all beings, all entities, all shapes of substances are compounds, and compounds are subject to dissolution. The immortal is not as you have it smaller than small and greater than great; it is neither small nor great; it is unsubstantial and without bodily shape. The immortal consists in the eternal verities by which existence is swayed; it is the immutable law of life the cognition of which constitutes enlightenment. The highest verities are the four noble truths, of misery, the origin of misery, the escape from misery, and the eightfold path of righteousness, which leads to the escape from misery."

Said Subhûti: "I grant that the eternal cannot be a material thing; the eternal cannot be a compound; it must be immaterial; it is spiritual. The self is not the body, not the senses, not the mind, not the intellect; it is that by which man perceives all objects in sleep or in waking. The consciousness 'I am' is the great omnipresent Self, which is bodiless within the body, as agni, the fire, lies hidden in the two fire sticks."

Anuruddha paid close attention to Subhûti's expositions, and replied in quick repartee: "Agni, the fire, does not lie hidden in the two fire sticks. The two fire sticks are wood, nothing but wood; and there is no fire hidden in either stick. The fire originates through the friction produced by your hands. In the same way consciousness originates as a product of conditions and disappears when the conditions cease. When the wood is burnt, whither does the fire go? And when the conditions of consciousness cease, where does consciousness abide?"

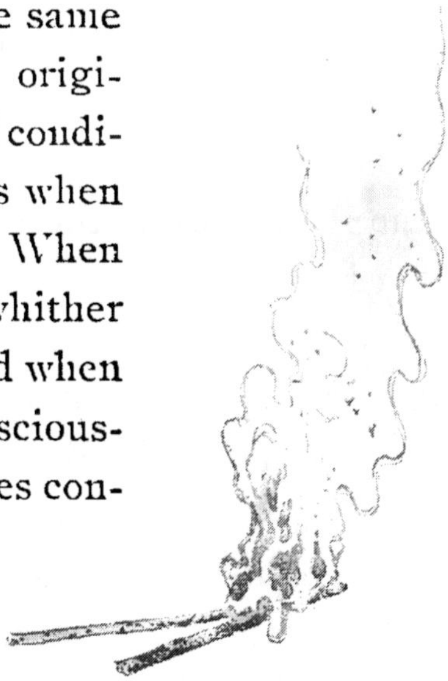

"My friend," said Subhûti, "we must distinguish between the thing and its phenomenon; between Agni and the flame; between consciousness and its manifestations; between the person and the properties of a person, his faculties or activities; between the wind and the commotion which the wind creates."

"Must we?" asked musingly the Brahman chief's guest. "It is true, we are in the habit of saying 'the wind blows,' as if there were the wind performing the action of blowing; but there are not two things: first the wind, and then the act of b'owing; there is only one thing, which is the motion of the air, called wind, or, by a license of speech, we speak of the blowing of the wind. In the same way there is not a person that remembers deeds, but the memories of the deeds are themselves the person."

"When a man is dead," enjoined Subhûti, "some say he exists, and others he exists not. I understand that the Blessed One teaches that he no longer exists, which means, to put it squarely, that there is no hereafter."

"No, sir," Anuruddha answered almost sharply: "No, sir. Your dilemma rests upon a wrong premise. That Self of yours does not now exist, how then can it continue to exist after you have gone? That, however, which you are now, will persist after the termination of your bodily existence. Truly you are right when you compare man in your Katha-Upanishad to that ancient tree whose roots grow upward and whose branches grow downward. As the tree reappears with all the characteristics of its kind, so man is reincarnated, and his peculiar karma is reborn in new individuals. There is no Self in the fig-tree that migrates from the parent stem to the new shoots, but the type in all its individual features is preserved in the further growth and in the evolution of new trees."[15]

"There is one eternal thinker," said Subhûti, "thinking non-eternal thoughts, and the eternal thinker is the Self."

"Would not your statement be truer," interrupted Anuruddha, "if reversed: there are eternal thoughts which are thought by non-eternal thinkers? In other words, what we call a thinker is but the thinking of the thought; and the thinking of true thoughts is the attainment of the eternal. The Truth is the Immortal, the truth is Nirvâna."

There was a lull in the conversation and after a pause the Buddhist monk continued:

"Your Katha-Upanishad is a discourse on the problem; it is a formulation of the How[16] as to the hereafter, but instead of giving an answer, it merely builds up a beautiful air-castle. The true solution is only given in the doctrine of the Tathâgata."

The Brahman chief felt that his most sacred convictions were omitted in this statement, and he asked, not without a tremor of uneasiness in his voice: "Is there nothing in me that is immutable, nothing that is eternal and immortal?"

"Whether or not there is anything immortal in you," was Anuruddha's reply, "depends solely upon yourself. If you consist of thoughts that are pure and holy, you are pure and holy; if you consist of thoughts that are sinful, you are sinful; and if you consist of immortal truth, you are immortal. The attainment of truth is immortality, and to do the work of truth is Nirvâna."

Subhûti shook his head. "I want to possess the truth, but I do not want to lose my own identity."

"And I," enjoined Anuruddha, "want the

truth to possess me so as to lose myself in the cause of the Truth. What a blessing it is to have a higher purpose in life than self!"

Subhûti gazed at his friend in amazement: "What shall I be after the dissolution of my body in death? I shrink from losing my Self. Should there be nothing that I can call my own?"

"Let my reply," rejoined Anuruddha, "be in the words of the Blessed One, who said:

"'Naught follows him who leaves this life;
For all things must be left behind:
Wife, daughters, sons, one's kin, and friends,
Gold, grain, and wealth of every kind.
But every deed a man performs,
With body, or with voice, or mind,
'Tis this that he can call his own,
This will he never leave behind.

"'Deeds, like a shadow, ne'er depart:
Bad deeds can never be concealed;
Good deeds cannot be lost and will
In all their glory be revealed.
Let all, then, noble deeds perform,
As seeds sown in life's fertile field;
For merit gained this life within,
Rich blessings in the next will yield.'"[17]

Having quoted the words of the Blessed One, Anuruddha continued: "Your deeds are your own and will remain your own forever and aye. Your thoughts, your words, your actions are not gone when they are past; they stay with you. They are the living stones of which the structure of your being is built up. And there is no power in heaven nor upon earth, nor even in hell, by which you can get rid of them. Your life-history is your Self, your actual self, and as your life-history continues after your death, so your identical self will remain. When we pass away we shall continue to live according to our deeds."

THE EPIDEMIC.

THREE children were born to the young couple, and all three were boys full of promise. Sudatta's prospects were brighter than he had ever dared to hope. But times change and misfortunes overcome men sometimes when least expected. A drought set in, which dried up all the wells of the country, spreading famine and contagious disease. The people prayed to the gods, they fasted and expiated their sins, the priests offered sacrifices and recited incantations, but the rain did not fall. More sacrifices were offered, and the blood of slaughtered animals reeked to heaven; yet the drought continued; the gods remained deaf to the prayers of the priests; the famine became worse, and the disease caused more ravage than before.

Subhûti, the chief, did all he could to alleviate the sorry lot of his afflicted people. He was a rich man, but his wealth proved insufficient to feed the poor.

Sudatta did his best in ministering unto the sick. Having learned from his father, the village priest whose office it was to gather the sacred herbs for sacrifices, the virtues of various plants, he brewed medicinal drinks for assuaging the sufferings of the patients and he was aided in his work by Subhûti his noble father-in-law and Kacchâyana, his brother-in-law.

When at last the epi-

demic began to abate, it came to pass that Subhûti the chief himself fell sick. At first it seemed that he was merely exhausted through

night-watches and grief, but soon it became apparent that he was affected by the disease and his condition grew very critical. His relatives gathered at his bedside and were inconsolable.

He had been so faithful in his kindness to every one that they thought they could not live without him; but he himself remained serene and self-possessed. Having blessed his sons, his daughter, and grand-children, he comforted them, saying: "Cease sorrowing; there is no loss in this body of flesh; it is outworn by old age and disease like a garment. If you cherish with faithful hearts the example that I set you, death can never separate us."

When the evening came, Subhûti sent away his daughter and grand-children, keeping only Kacchâyana and Sudatta with him. And when the pain of the disease for a while abated, he said: "The sufferings which I witnessed opened mine eyes and I have understood the four noble truths proclaimed by the Tathâgata. I feel that my life is ebbing away, but I am not troubled in my mind, for death has lost its terrors. Wherever I shall be reborn, I am confident that it will be on a higher plane and I shall be a step nearer the holy goal Nirvâna."

"Surely, father," rejoined Sudatta, "after a long life spent in doing good, thou deservest a high reward, which will be nothing less than the bliss of Brahma's heaven."

Rallying all his strength once more, Subhûti replied: "Speak not of rewards while there are duties to be performed. Brahma's heaven is made for those who cling to the thought of Self. I am confident that this present incarnation of mine shall have peace; but not my love for mankind; not my sympathy with those who suffer; not my truth-seeking mind. So long as there is suffering in the world I shall never entertain any desire to ascend into a heaven of bliss; I want to be reborn in the depths of hell. There the misery is greatest and salvation most needed. That is the best place to enlighten those in darkness, to rescue what is lost, and to point out the path to those who have gone astray."

With these words Subhûti fell back exhausted. He murmured with a broken voice the refuge formula of the Buddhists, saying:

"I take my refuge in the Buddha,
I take my refuge in the Dharma,
I take my refuge in the Sangha."

Having thus given expression to the faith that was in him, his eyes, which had just before been sparkling with noble enthusiasm, grew dim, and he passed away peacefully.

A holy stillness pervaded the room.

* * *

And it happened that very evening that Anuruddha passed through Kuduraghara and when he came to the mansion of Subûhti he found his friend the chief no longer among the living. He saluted Kacchâyana and Sudatta and sat down with them in silence.

The sun sank down and Kacchâyana lit a candle, but no one spoke a word.

When the night advanced Anuruddha raised his sonorous voice and sang:

"How transient are things mortal!
How restless is man's life!
But Peace stands at the portal
Of Death, and ends all strife.

"Life is a constant parting—
One more the stream has crossed;
But think ye who stand smarting
Of that which ne'er is lost.

"All rivers flowing, flowing,
Must reach the distant main;
The seeds which we are sewing
Will ripen into grain."[18]

COPYING THE MANUSCRIPT.

KACCHÂYANA joined Anuruddha on his journey to Râjagaha, and when he saw the Blessed One and heard him explain the doctrine, he entered the order of samanas and became a man of repute among them on account of his wisdom. When he returned home he retired into the forest near Kuduragghara to a place called the Precipice, and the people of his village called him Mahâ-Kacchâyana,[19] for although they, being Brahmans, looked upon him as a heretic, they respected him and said: "He is one of the great disciples of the Blessed One, well versed in both, the Brahman and Buddhist Scriptures, and we know that he has attained the highest degree of scholarship and sanctity."

Sudatta had lost his faith in the religion of his fathers, without, however, adopting the new faith of the Buddhists. One day, when walking with his brother-in-law through the village, he said: "Is it not sad to lose a father or any one whom we dearly love? Truly there is no doctrine that can take away the pangs of grief and afford genuine comfort."

"My dear brother," replied Kacchâyana, "so long as your aim is to escape suffering for your own person, you are not yet free. Let the pain of your grief have its way, and do not try to be exempt from the natural law to which all mortals are subject alike."

"But consider," objected the other one, "the terrible fate of the dead. Is it not an awful thought that their whole existence is wiped out as if they had never been?"

"There you are mistaken," suggested Kacchâyana. Death is a dissolution, but man's existence is not wiped out as though he had never been, for every deed of his continues in its peculiar identity."

A sad smile appeared on Sudatta's face when he interrupted his brother-in-law: "That is nothing more than a mode of speech. If the dead continue to live, please tell me where is our father now?"

Kacchâyana replied: "Is he not here with us?" And after a pause he continued: "It is with men as with books. You can write vile things or good and noble thoughts upon palm leaves. The book does not consist of leaves but of ideas. The leaves are mere material for the scribe, and there are thousands of leaves on the palms that will never be turned into books. When our father, the venerable Subhûti, pondered over the problem of death, he composed the Katha-Upanishad which appeared to me more valuable than any one I had ever heard or read. He wrote it upon the leaves of the big palm-tree in our garden. When the leaves were bleached and prepared for writing, our venerable father scratched the words of the Upanishad into the leaves, and when he died left them to me as my most precious inheritance, for they are not treasures of worldly goods, but a monument of his meditations which contains his immortal soul. Formerly I held them dear because I valued them as a specimen of his hand-writing, but now I deem his thoughts to be of higher worth. During the great drought the leaves became worm-eaten, and they are now breaking to pieces. I have the whole Upanishad in my memory, but knowing that when I die the thoughts expressed in the book will be lost, I have begun to transcribe them, line by line, carefully, from the rotten leaves of the old manuscript. I shall lend the new copy to other scribes, and the Katha-Upanishad will be preserved and become known in other lands and to other generations. The old copy has become illegible and has partly crumbled into dust, but the thoughts will not die, for they are re-embodied in the new copy. It is in this same way that we, our aspirations, our ideas, our mind, will be preserved. The character of the present generation is impressed upon the coming generation by our acts, our words, and our sentiments, and when we die we pass away but continue according to our deeds. All that is compounded must be dissolved again; the palm-leaves wither, but the Katha-Upanishad still lives."

"Would it not be glorious," exclaimed Sudatta, "if both could be preserved—the copy of the book and the thought contained in it?"

"I would hesitate to echo your sentiment," rejoined Kacchâyana: "Do you remember the beautiful words of Anuruddha which found an echo in that same Upanishad? He said: 'Choose not the dearer, choose the truer, for the truer is the better.' At that time I chose the dearer, but life has taught me a lesson; I have now chosen the truer, and the truer has become the dearer to me."

"Has it, indeed?" queried Sudatta, without concealing his surprise.

"Indeed it has," was Kacchâyana's reply. "Death is not only necessary in life, as the inevitable corollary of birth, but it is also a most salutary arrangement. There is no more reason to speak of the horrors of death than to speak of the horrors of sleep. Indeed there is a beauty in death; and it is the beauty of death that lends consecration to life. Think only of what life would be without death; a monotonous and thoughtless sporting in pleasures and nothing more. It is death that makes time precious. Death sets us to thinking and makes religion necessary. Death alone forces us to give value to life. If there were no death, there would be no heroes, no sages, no Buddhas. Therefore, death is inevitable; yet it is not an evil. Fools shudder at the mere thought of it; but the wise fear it not. For death is our teacher, and also our benefactor."

YOUNG SUBHÛTI.

SUDATTA'S boys grew up and took charge of the land that they had inherited from their grandfather. Their assistance made it possible for Sudatta to gain more leisure for himself, and he began frequently to retire to the Precipice, in the loneliness of the forest, where Kacchâyana lived, and devoted himself to study and meditation. Although only in the forties, his hair had turned white and he might easily have passed for an older man, who, however, in his old age, preserved unusual vigor and health. The people of the village called him whenever there was sickness in the family, and he was always willing to help them in their troubles with counsel and personal assistance.

In those days it came to pass that Bimbisâra, the king, died, and his son Ajâtasattu ascended the throne.

Ajâtasattu sent envoys to all the cities and villages of his kingdom and also to all the neighboring countries that were subject to his sceptre, to test the allegiance of his people. And the King's envoy, surrounded by a staff of counsellors and accompanied by a military

escort, came also to Kuduraghara. When they entered Kuduraghara they were told, on inquiring for the chief of the village, that since the death of Mahâ-Subhûti the people had been living without a chief. Then the King's envoy

had the people assembled, and requested them to choose a new magistrate whom the King,

Ajâtasattu, should install in the place of Mahâ-Subhûti. Seeing that Kacchâyana had retired from the world to live a religious life, and that Sudatta appeared to be quite advanced in years, he presented as a candidate Sudatta's oldest son who was called Subhûti after his grandfather; and when the people saw him in his manliness they hailed him and shouted, "Let young Subhûti be our chief; let the King appoint him successor to Mahâ-Subhûti."

Some of the older men in the assembly were greatly pleased with the new chief and said: "If Mahâ-Subhûti were to reappear bodily among us in the vigor of his youth, he could not look different from this noble youth. Mahâ-Subhûti was exactly like him when King Bimbisâra installed him in office."

THE BLESSED ONE.

ONE day a stranger passed through Kuduraghara, and, meeting Sudatta in the street, asked him the road to Râjagaha. The old Brahman pointed out the way to the capital of the country, and said: "I should like to go to Râjagaha myself, for there the Blessed One lives, the Holy Buddha, who is the teacher of gods and men. He is the master whose doctrine I profess."

"Why not join me?" said the stranger. "I am Chandra, the gambler. Having heard of the wisdom of the Blessed Buddha, I made up my mind to go to Râjagaha and reap the benefits of his instruction."

Sudatta took leave of his friends and joined Chandra, the gambler, on his way to Râjagaha, and, remembering a wish once uttered by his father-in-law, he took with him the palm-leaf manuscript of the Katha-Upanishad.

While they were travelling together on the highroad, Chandra said: "Deep is the wis-

dom of the Perfect One. He teaches that existence is suffering, and my experience confirms the doctrine. Pessimism is indeed the true theory of life."

"What do you mean by Pessimism?" interrupted Sudatta.

"Pessimism means that the world is bad," replied Chandra; and he continued: "The world is like a lottery in which there are few prizes and innumerable blanks. We can see at once how true it is that life is not worth living by supposing a wealthy man buying all the chances in a lottery in order to make sure of winning all the prizes. He would certainly be a loser. Life is bankrupt throughout; it is like a business enterprise which does not pay its expenses."

"My friend," said the Brahman, "I perceive that you are a man of experience. Am I right in assuming that, being a gambler, you had for a time an easy life until you met another gambler better versed in trickery than yourself, who cheated you out of all your possessions?"

"Indeed, sir," said the gambler, "that is my case exactly; and now I travel to the Blessed One, who has recognised the great truth that life is like a lost game in which the prizes are only baits for the giddy. Whenever I met a man unacquainted with gambling I always let him win in the beginning to make him bold. I, too, was for a time successful in the game of life, but now I know that those who win at first are going to lose more in the end than those who are frightened away by losing their first stake. Life uses the same tricks we use. I have been caught in the snare which I thought I had invented."

Turning to the Brahman, bent with age and care, he continued: "The whiteness of your beard and the wrinkles in your face indicate that you, too, have found the sweets of life bitter. I suppose you are not less pessimistic than myself."

A beam of sunshine appeared in the Brahman's eyes and his gait became erect like that of a king. "No, sir," he replied, "I have no experience like yours. I tasted the sweets of life when I was young, many, many years ago. I have sported in the fields with my playmates. I have loved and was beloved, but I loved with a pure heart and there was no bitterness in the sweets which I tasted. My experience came when I saw the sufferings of life. The world is full of sorrow and the end of life is death. I have been sad at heart ever since, but when I think of the Buddha who has come into the world and teaches us how to escape suffering I rejoice; I know now that the bitterness of life is sweet to him whose soul has found rest in Nirvâna."

"If life is full of bitterness, how can one escape suffering?" asked Chandra.

And Sudatta replied: "We cannot escape pain, but we can avoid evil, and it is by avoiding evil we enter Nirvâna."

When the two men came to the Vihâra at Râjagaha they approached the Blessed Buddha with clasped hands, saying: "Receive us, O Lord, among thy disciples; permit us to be hearers of thy doctrines; and let us take refuge in the Buddha, the truth, and the community of Buddha's followers."

And the Holy One, who reads the secret thoughts of men's minds, addressed Chandra, the gambler, asking him: "Knowest thou, O Chandra, the doctrine of the Blessed One?"

Chandra said: "I do. The Blessed One teaches that life is misery."

And the Lord replied: "Life is misery indeed, but the Tathâgata hast come into the world to point out the way of salvation. His aim is to

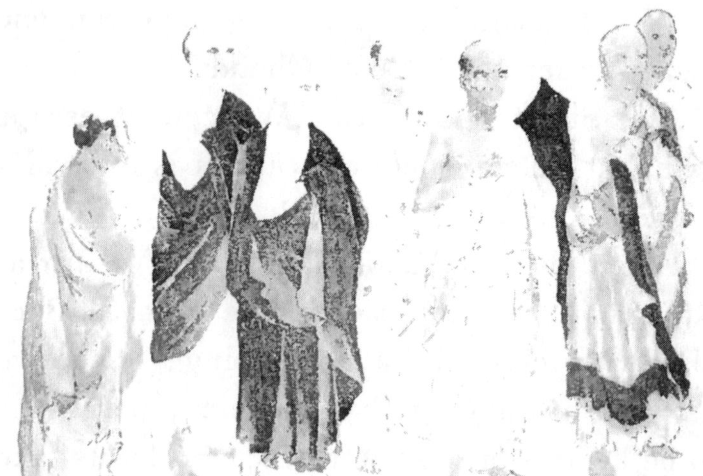

teach men how to rescue themselves from misery. If thou art anxious for deliverance from evil, enter the path with a resolute mind, sur-

render selfishness, practise self-discipline, and work out thy salvation with diligence."

"I came to the Blessed One to find peace," said the gambler, "not to undertake work."

Said the Blessed One: "Only by energetic work can peace be found; death can be conquered only by the resignation of self, and only by strenuous effort is eternal bliss attained. Thou regardest the world as evil because he who deceives will eventually be ruined by his own devices. The happiness that thou seekest is the pleasure of sin without sin's evil consequences. Men who have not observed proper discipline, and have not gained treasure in their youth, lie sighing for the past. There is evil, indeed; but the evil of which thou complainest is but the justice of the law of karma. What a man has sown that shall he reap."

Then the Blessed One turned to the Brahman, and, recognising the sterling worth of his character, addressed him: "Verily, O Brahman, thou understandest the doctrines of the Tathâgata better than thy fellow-traveller. He who makes the distress of others his own, quickly understands the illusion of self. He is like the lotus flower that grows in the water, yet does the water not wet its petals. The pleasures of this world allure him not, and he will have no cause for regret."

Searching with a friendly eye the benevolent features of his Brahman visitor, the Buddha continued: "Thou art walking in the noble path of righteousness and thou delightest in the purity of thy work. If thou wishest to cure the diseases of the heart, as thou understandest how to heal the sores of the body, let people see the fruits that grow from the seeds of loving kindness. When they but know the bliss of a right mind they will soon enter the path and reach that state of steadiness and tranquillity in which they are above pleasure and pain, above the petty petulance of fretful desires, above sin and temptation. Go, then, back to thy home and announce to thy friends, who are subject to suffering, that he whose mind is free from the illusions of sinful desires will overcome the miseries of life. Spread goodness in words and deeds everywhere. In a spirit of universal kindness be ready to serve others with help and instruction; live happily, then, among the ailing;

among men who are greedy, remain free from greed; among men who hate, dwell free from hatred; and those who witness the blessings of a holy life will follow thee in the path of salvation."

Chandra listened with rapture to the words of the Blessed One and exclaimed: "Happy

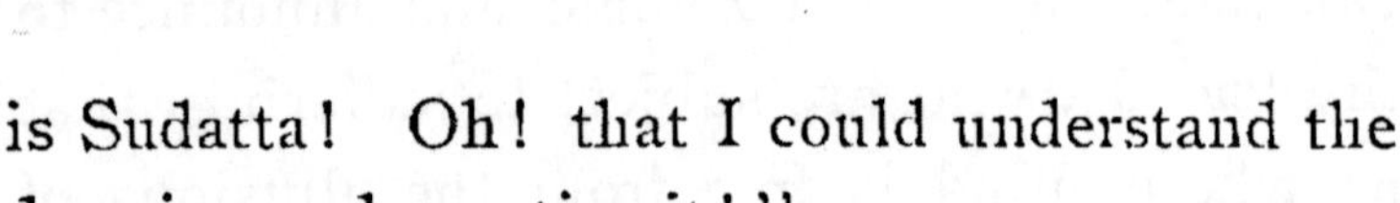

is Sudatta! Oh! that I could understand the doctrine and practice it!"

The Blessed One said: "As the great ocean has only one taste, the taste of salt, so the doctrine of the Tathâgata has only one taste, the taste of salvation.

The eyes of the gambler were opened, and

his pessimism melted away in the sun of Buddha's doctrines. "O Lord," said he, "I long for that higher life to which the noble path of righteousness leads."

Said the Blessed One: "As sea-faring men are bent on reaching the haven of their destination, so all life presses forward to find the

bliss of enlightenment, and enlightenment alone can point out the way of righteousness that leads to Nirvâna."

The gambler folded his hands and said to the Buddha: "Wilt thou persuade the Brahman, my fellow-traveller, to take me to his home, where I am willing to enter his service that I may learn from him and attain to the same bliss?"

The Blessed One replied: "Let Sudatta the Brahman, do as he sees fit."

Sudatta, the Brahman, expressed his willingness to receive Chandra as a helpmate in his work, and added: "Anurudha the philosopher taught me the path of the Dharma, which proclaims: 'Let evil deeds be covered by good deeds; he who was reckless and becomes sober, will brighten up the world like the moon when freed from clouds.'"

Seeing that the hearts of all present were ready to receive the good tidings of salvation, the Blessed One instructed them and roused and gladdened them with religious discourse, and having explained the doctrine, he concluded his sermon saying: "And this is the sign that you have reached the goal which is the glorious Nirvâna: No accident will ever be able to disturb your mind, for, in spite of the world's unrest, your heart will be like a still and smooth lake. All attachment to Self has died out; it has become like a withered branch that no longer bears fruit. But your sympathy goes out to every creature that suffers, and you are untiring in good works. Your heart beats higher; it expands and is roused to a nobler life; for it is inspired by the thoughts of the Buddha; your mind is clearer, for it now comprehends the length, the breadth, and the depth of existence, recognising the one goal that life must seek,—Nirvâna."

NOTES.

1, Page 1

The names and terms which occur in this little tale are as a rule transcriptions from the Pâli, exceptions being made only in the case of such words as have in their Sanskrit forms become naturalised in the English language; for instance, Nirvâna, Dharma, Karma, etc., which are better known than their analogous Pâli forms: Nibbâna, Dhamma, Kamma.

2, Page 3.

Kuduraghara is mentioned by Buddhaghosha and other authors. In the Mahâvagga (V, 13) it is spelt Kuraraghara. Avanti is the present Malwa, the country north of the Vindhya mountains and southwest of the middle course of the Ganges. See e. g., the Map of Nobir Chandra Das in his "Note on the Ancient Geography of Asia."

3, Page 7.

See *Chulla Vagga*, V., 6; compare C. H. Warren, *Buddhism in Translations*, pp. 302–303.

4, Page 10.

From the *Sainkhapâla jâtaka* (Birth Story 316). See Warren. *B. in Tr.*, p. 274.

5, Page 10.

Bodhisatta (Sanskrit *Bodhisattva*), i. e., he whose essence (*sattva*) is enlightenment (*bodhi*), is the title of Buddha before he attained Buddhahood.

6, Page 18.

Gautama, the Sanskrit form of Buddha's family name (to be pronounced "Goutama"), is here preferred to the Pâli *Gotamo* because we have become as much accustomed to it as to the form Buddha. Buddha is called Gautama by unbelievers only, and Buddhists deem it irreverent to call their master by his family name simply. They call him Tathâgata (which probably means the Perfect One), or Sâkya Muni, the Sage of the Sâkya tribe, or Bhagavat, the Blessed One, etc.

7, Page 19.

Anuruddha is one of the great disciples of the Buddha.

8, Page 28.

The marriage ceremonies of India are described by Dr. M Winternitz in *Das altindische Hochzeitsrituell nach dem Apastambiya-Grihyasûtra*, Vienna, 1892. Concerning the Brâhma-rite see the Laws of Manu, III, 25.

9, Page 32.

Anattavâdo should by right have been the title of this story. The word was suggested to me by the Pâli scholar Mr. Albert J. Edmunds, and it means non-assertion of self, from *an*, the negation, *attâ*=self, and *vâdo*=assertion. (See Childers's *Dictionary of the Pâli Language*, s v. *attâ*=atman, *attavâdo* and *vâdo*). The non-assertion of self is an entry into Nirvâna in this life.

While *anattavâdo* is an abrogation of all selfishness, an attainment of enlightenment and peace of mind, it is by no means quietism; on the contrary, it implies extraordinary effort in behalf of every worthy aim of life that might fall to one's lot to pursue. No founder of any other religion insisted more earnestly upon energetic and resolute exertion than the Buddha.

10, Page 33.

From the Mahâmangala Sutta, the Buddhist Beatitudes, a translation of which is contained in Rhys Davids's *Buddhism*, pp. 125–126. Compare also Sir Monier Monier-Williams's translation.

11, Page 34.

The Vedânta philosophy in speculating on psychological problems hypostasised the soul under the name self or âtman, and Prof. F. Max Müller proposed to translate âtman by "Self," capitalised with a plural form "Selfs," to distinguish the term from the pronouns "myself" and "ourselves," etc. The peculiarity of the Vedântic explanation is the fiction of a separate Self which is assumed to be immutable and eternal.

12, Page 34.

Îshvara (literally "independent existence") is an appellative of Shiva, but it is always used in Buddhist literature in the sense of "personal god," i. e., an extra-mundane and anthropomorphic deity endowed with an individual ego-consciousness.

13, Page 35.

Sudatta's attack of Buddhism is a condensed statement of the criticism made in ancient times by Buddha's opponents, and the same objections have been repeated ever since, down to the present day.

14, Page 42.

We recommend the perusal of the Katha-upanishad, translated by F. M. Müller in the *Sacred Books of the East*, XV., pp. 1–24, and by Deussen in his *Sechzig Upanishads*, pp. 266–287. Among other translations Sir Edwin Arnold's and Charles Johnston's versions are more readable because they excel in literary beauty.

The Kathas constitute the school of the Black Yajurveda (a book of sacrificial rituals), and the Katha-upanishad is a poetical discourse based upon the fire ceremonial. Cf. Weber's *History of Indian Literature*, p. 93 *et passim*. The Katha school is still in the present day the prevailing one in Kashmir (Weber, *ibid.*, p. 317).

The Upanishads are an important branch of the philosophical literature of ancient India. They represent the transition from Brahmanism to Buddhism, and the Katha-Upanishad is perhaps the most beautiful of all.

The solution of the soul-problem offered in the Upanishads is that of the Vedânta philosophy; it is the belief in a Self or âtman which is supposed to be a separate entity, assumed to be no bigger than the thumb, or even as small as a mustard-seed. While all things change, this Self is supposed to remain immutable. Buddha denies the existence of an âtman, whence originated the accusation that he teaches there is no soul.

The Katha-Upanishad must have originated in some such way as is related in our story. The argument in the text refers to an ancient fire ritual and at the same time shows, as do some other Upanishads, Buddhist influences. Yet the philosophical tenor of the discussion is still Brahmanical, being pervaded by the same spirit that finds its classical expression in Shankara's philosophy.

15. Page 53.

Here the keynote of Buddhist psychology is touched. The Anguttara Nikâyo (III, 134, 1.) teaches as an essential doctrine, taught by the Blessed One himself, that the constituents of being (viz., the elements of concrete existence, such as build up all things including our own personality) possess three characteristics: they are (1) transitory, (2) subject to suffering, and (3) lacking an âtman, i.e., a Self or Ego. This means (1) that all compounds must finally be dissolved again. Things (including organisms and the personality of man) originate by composition and, be they ever so stable, they will finally decay and die. (2) The life of organisms, in so far as it is sentient, is capable of enjoying pleasure, but is necessarily subject to pain. Thus suffering is not an accessory but an inevitable characteristic of life. (3) The thing consists of parts, and there is no Self (no ego, no âtman) in addition to these parts; or as modern philosophers would say now, there is no thing in itself. The Ganges consists of water and its banks. If we take the banks away and the water, the Ganges is gone. There is no Ganges in itself.

The truth that after all lies in the conception of things-in-themselves, may be briefly expressed in the statement: "There are no things-in themselves but forms-in-themselves, viz., eternal types such as are called by Plato the ideas," (cf. the author's article in *The Monist*, Vol. II., No. 2 pp. 225-265, "Are There Things-in-Themselves?").

Judging from the doctrine of the three characteristics alone, Buddhism seems to be pessimism. But this is not so. Buddha has pointed out the way of salvation which consists in the attainment of Nirvâna; and Nirvâna can be attained in this life by abandoning all attachment to the transitory and finding a resting-place in the eternal. We read in the Udâna (VIII, 3):

"There is, O disciples, something not-born, not-originated, not-made, not-formed. If, O disciples, there were not this not-born, not-originated, not-made, not-formed, there would be no escape for the born, the originated, the made, the formed."

Compare also *Dhammapada*, Chapter XXVI., verse 383, quoted as a motto on the title page.

The nature of this "not-born, not-originated, not-made, not-formed" is sufficiently explained in our tale by Anuruddha.

16, Page 54.

Here Anuruddha makes a play at words, of which the ancient Indians were very fond. There are three words which differ slightly in pronunciation. (1) Ka*th*a (with lingual *th*) the name of the founder of the Ka*th*a school; (2) Kathâ (with dental *th* and long *â*), a discourse; and (3) Kathaṃ (with dental *th* and short *a*), the interrogative "How?"

17, Page 55.

After the Samyutta-Nikâyo. See Warren, *Buddh. in Tr.*, p. 228.

18, Page 63.

After an old Buddhist song which is still used in Ceylon and Siam, quoted by Rhys Davids in his introduction to the Mahâ-Parinibbâna Sutta (*S. B. of the E.*, Vol. XI., pp. xlii-xliii) as follows:

"Ani*kk*â vata sa*m*khârâ uppâdavaya-dhammino
Uppa*gg*itvâ niru*ggh*anti tesa*m* vûpasamo sukho.

Yathâ vârivahâ pûrâ paripûrenti sâgara*m*
Evam eva ito dinna*m* petânam upakappati.

Ito dinnena yâpenti petâ kâlakatâ tahi*m*.

Unname udaka*m* va*tt*a*m* yathâ ninna*m* pavattati
Evam eva ito dinna*m* petâna*m* upakappati."

The rendering given in our story is fitted to the melody of Goethe's poem "The King of Thule." See the author's *Sacred Tunes for the Consecration of Life*, pp. 36–37.

19, Page 65.

That Kacchâyana of Kuduraghara (or Kuraraghara), who lived on the Precipice was called Mahâ-Kacchâyana is mentioned in the Mahâvagga (V. 13).